VIRGIL THOMSON

THE PLOW THAT BROKE THE PLAINS

for Brass Quintet

ED-3826
First Printing: November 1993

G. SCHIRMER, *Inc.*

DISTRIBUTED BY
HAL•LEONARD® CORPORATION
7777 W. BLUEMOUND RD. P.O. BOX 13819 MILWAUKEE, WI 53213

THE PLOW THAT BROKE THE PLAINS

I. Prelude

Virgil Thomson
(1936)
arranged by Jay Rozen

II. Cowboy Songs

"Houlihan," "Laredo," and "Git Along Little Doggies"

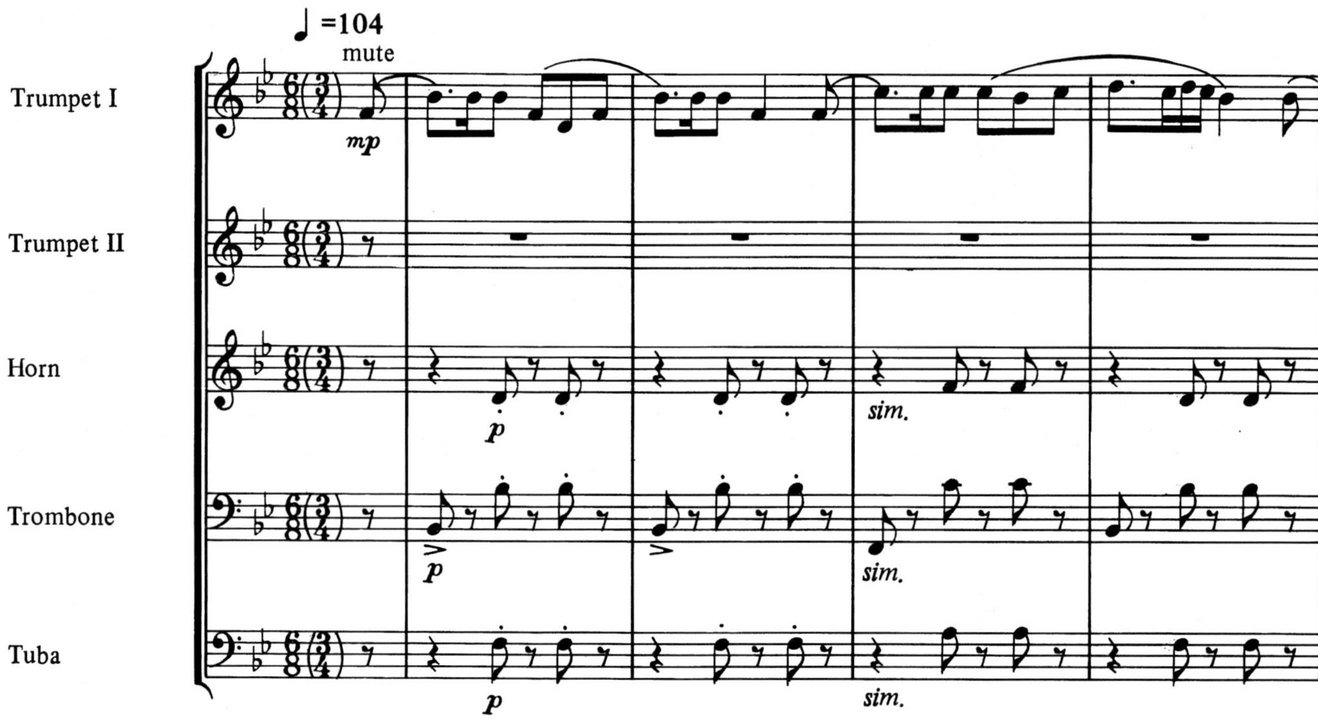

Tpt. I
Tpt. II
Hn.
Tbn.
Tuba
9
f
sim.
f
sim.
sim.
13
open
p
17
p
p
p
p
pp
pp

6

21
to E♭ Tpt.
Tpt. I
pp
p
Tpt. II
pp
p
Hn.
p
p
Tbn.
p
Tuba
pp
p

25
Tpt. I
Tpt. II
mp
Hn.
mp
mf
Tbn.
mp
Tuba
mp

29
E♭ Tpt.
Tpt. I
f
Tpt. II
Hn.
Tbn.
mf
Tuba
mf

33
Tpt. I
Tpt. II
Hn.
Tbn.
Tuba
mute
37
41
open

8.
45
Tpt. I
Tpt. II
Hn.
Tbn.
Tuba
49
Tpt. I
Tpt. II
Hn.
Tbn.
Tuba
53
Tpt. I
Tpt. II
Hn.
Tbn.
Tuba

69
Tpt. I
Tpt. II
Hn.
Tbn.
Tuba
ff
73
ff
mf
mf
ff
mf
ff
mf
p
ff
77
to Tpt. in B♭
rall.
p
p
p

III. Blues

♩ =96
plunger
open
Trumpet I
mp
p
Trumpet II
p
mp
Horn
p
Trombone
p
Tuba
p

5
plunger
open
Tpt. I
mp
p
ff
Tpt. II
p
mp
ff
Hn.
ff
Tbn.
ff
Tuba
f

Tpt. I
Tpt. II
Hn.
Tbn.
Tuba
plunger
open
9
12
15

19
Tpt. I
Tpt. II
Hn.
Tbn.
Tuba
gliss.
gliss.
gliss.
23
plunger
27

31
Tpt. I
Tpt. II
Hn.
Tbn.
Tuba
open
plunger
p
mp
35
open
plunger
open
p
mp
p
f
39
ff
f
f
f
p
p
p
p

42
Tpt. I
Tpt. II
Hn.
Tbn.
Tuba
sim.
sim.
sim.
46
Tpt. I
Tpt. II
Hn.
Tbn.
Tuba
fltg.
fltg.
fltg.
fp
sfz
fp
sf
fp
sfz
fp
fp
50
Tpt. I
Tpt. II
Hn.
Tbn.
Tuba
fltg.
fltg.
fltg.
fltg.
fltg.
fltg.
fltg.
fltg.
fltg.
fp
sfz
fp
sfz
fp
sfz
fp
sf
fp
sfz
fp
sfz
fp
sfz
fp
sfz
fp
sfz
fp
fp
fp
fp
fp
fp

53
Tpt. I
Tpt. II
Hn.
Tbn.
Tuba
fltg.
fp sfz
56
59

62
Tpt. I
Tpt. II
Hn.
Tbn.
Tuba
sim.
65
fff
ff
69
fp sfz

IV. Finale

"We're Goin' to Leave Ol' Texas Now"

9
Tpt. I
Tpt. II
Hn.
Tbn.
Tuba
p sub. dolce
p sub. dolce
p sub. dolce
p sub. dolce
p sub. dolce
p
13
Tpt. I
Tpt. II
Hn.
Tbn.
Tuba
17
Tpt. I
Tpt. II
Hn.
Tbn.
Tuba
p
p
p
p

rallentando
33
Tpt. I
Tpt. II
Hn.
Tbn.
Tuba
f
ff dim.
p
38
a tempo
42
mp
p

94
Tpt. I
Tpt. II
Hn.
Tbn.
Tuba
98
Tpt. I
Tpt. II
pp legato e dolce
Hn.
Tbn.
ppp
Tuba
102
Tpt. I
Tpt. II
Hn.
Tbn.
Tuba
pp

106
Un poco piu lento ♩ = 60
Tpt. I
Tpt. II
Hn.
Tbn.
Tuba
mf molto vib.
mf molto vibr.
mp
mp
mp
110
114
f
f
f
f
sim.
sim.
sim.

VIRGIL THOMSON

THE PLOW THAT BROKE THE PLAINS

for Brass Quintet

Trumpet 1

ED•3826
First Printing: November 1993

G. SCHIRMER, Inc.

THE PLOW THAT BROKE THE PLAINS

15
Tpt. 2
(open)
p
20
pp
p
to E♭ Tpt.
25
6
Tpt. 2
E♭ Tpt.
f
35
5
mf
f
42
f
47
3
ff
54
mp
59
p
p
mp
64
3
p
71
ff
mf
75
to Tpt. in B♭
3
rall.

Ⅲ. Blues

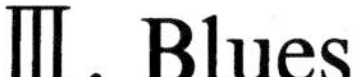

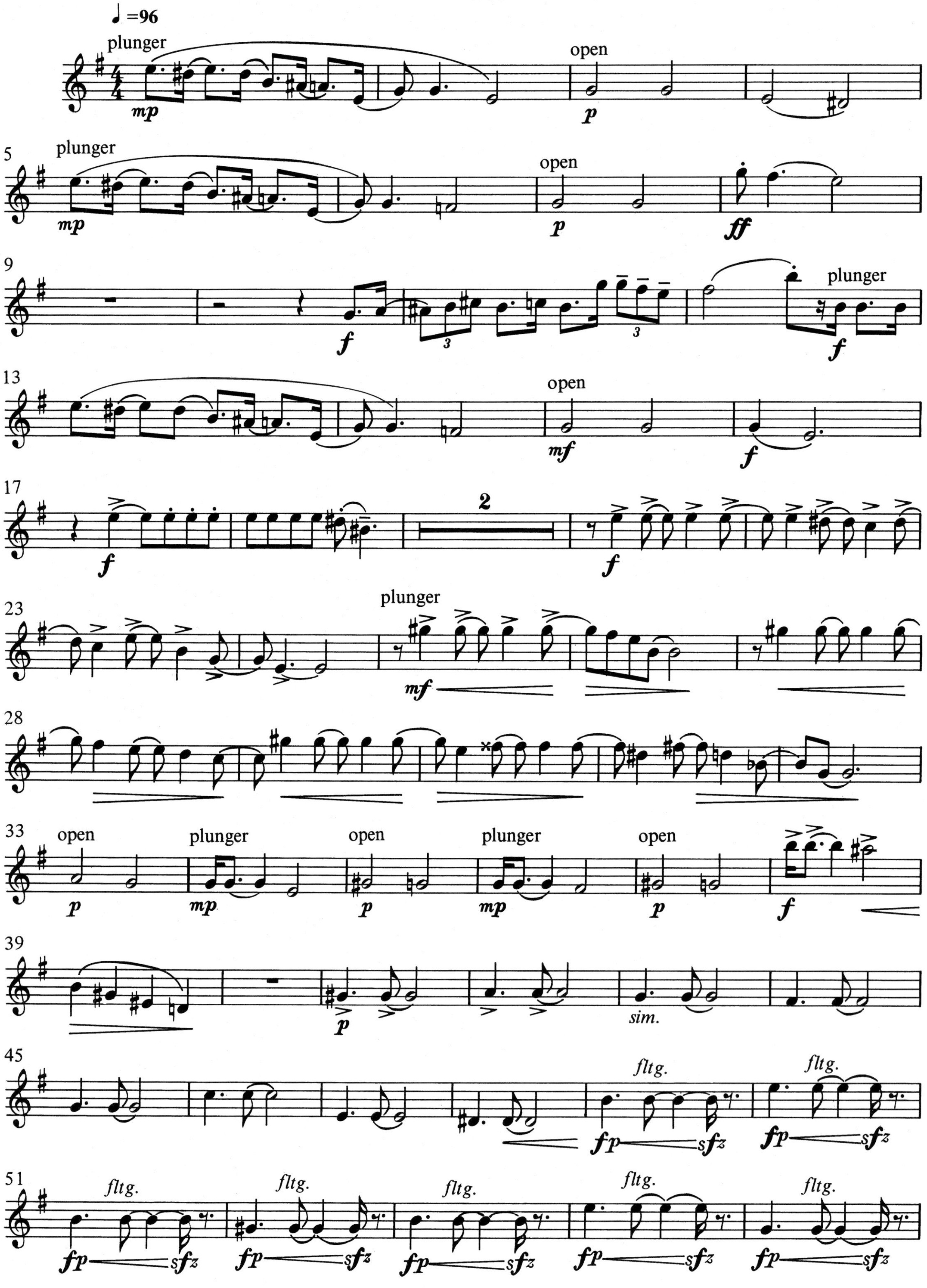
♩=96
plunger
mp
open
p
5
plunger
mp
open
p
ff
9
f
plunger
f
13
open
mf
f
17
f
2
f
23
plunger
mf
28
33
open
p
plunger
mp
open
p
plunger
mp
open
p
f
39
p
sim.
45
fltg.
fp
sfz
fltg.
fp
sfz
51
fltg.
fp
sfz
fltg.
fp
sfz
fltg.
fp
sfz
fltg.
fp
sfz
fltg.
fp
sfz

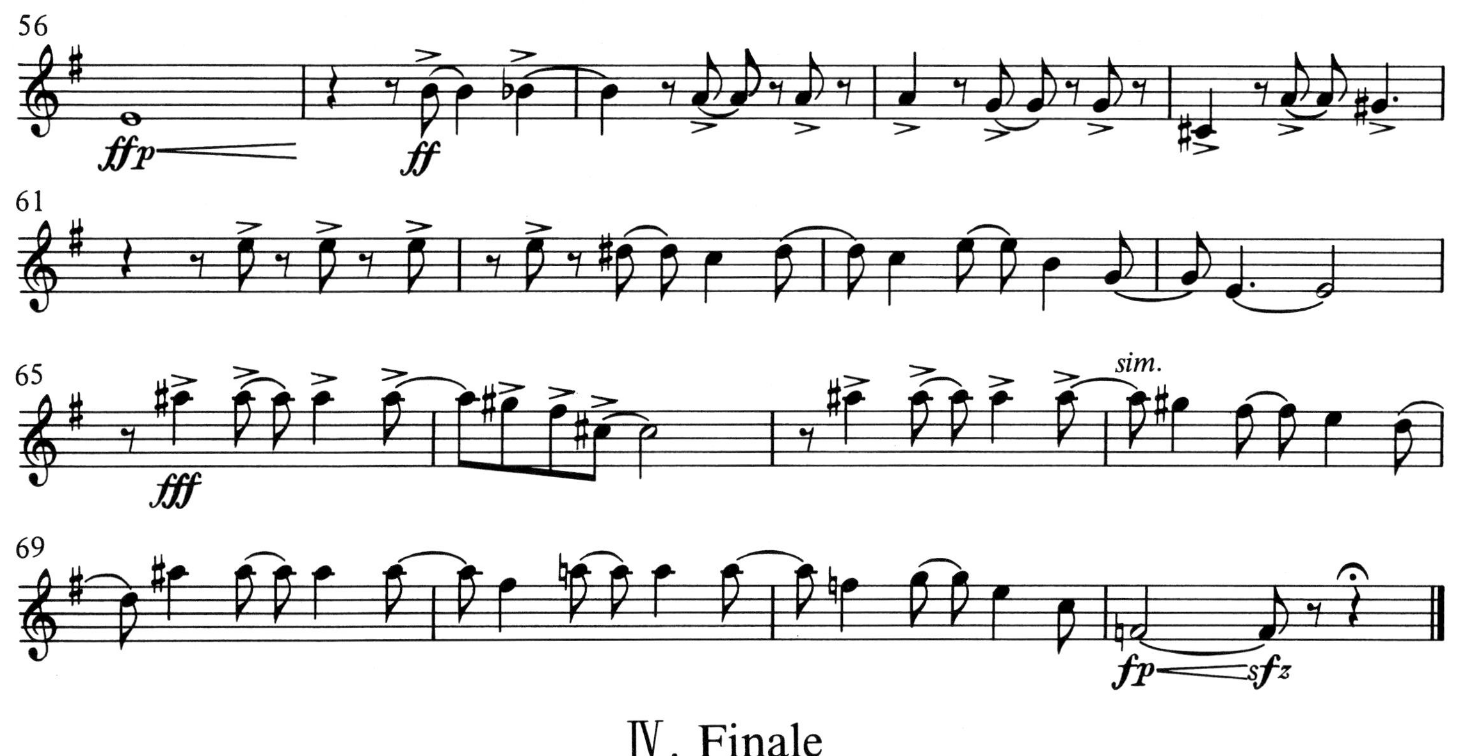

56
ffp
ff
61
65
fff
sim.
69
fp
sfz

IV. Finale

"We're Goin' to Leave Ol' Texas Now"

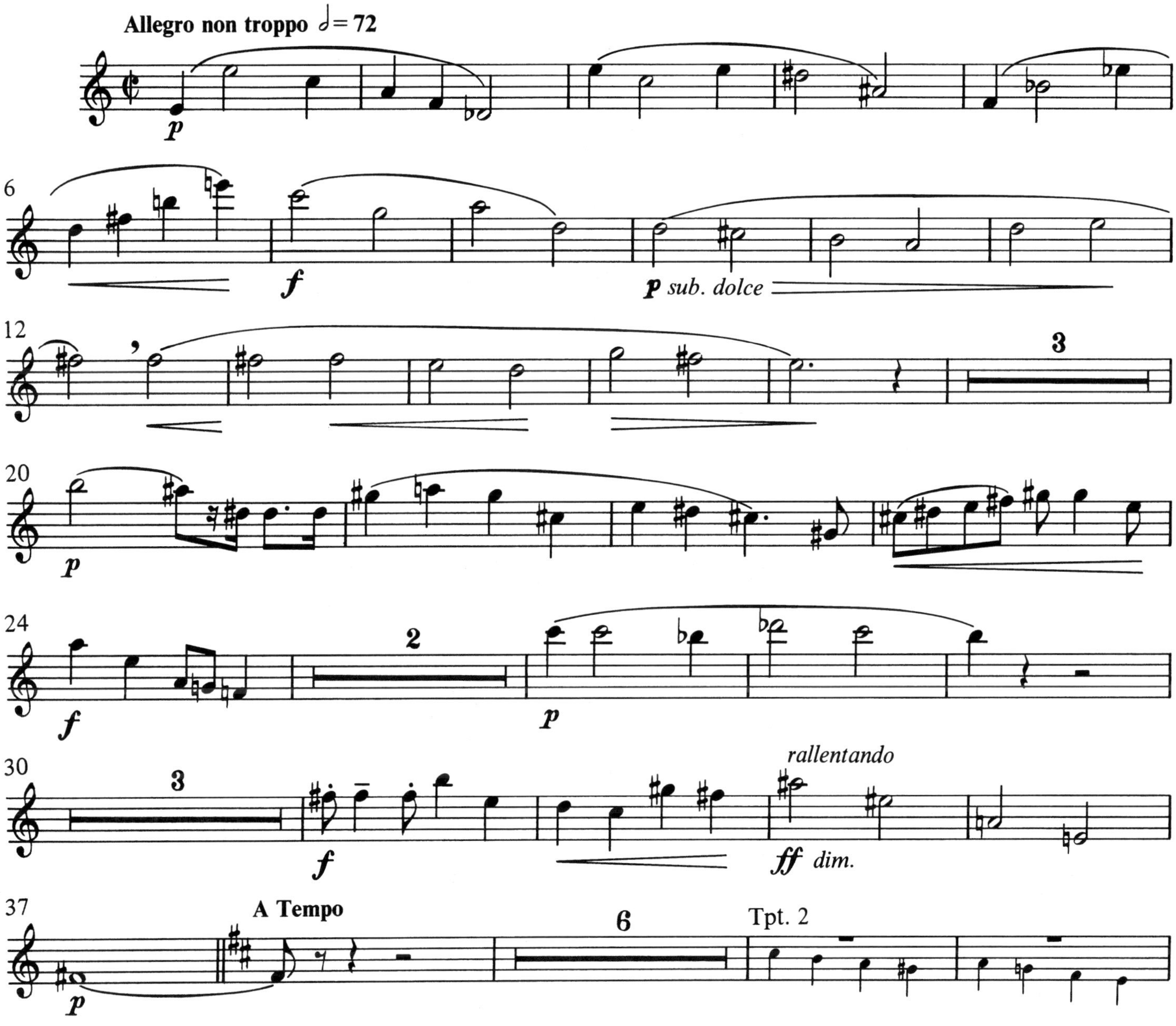
Allegro non troppo 𝅗𝅥 = 72
p
6
f
p sub. dolce
12
3
20
p
24
f
2
p
30
3
f
rallentando
ff dim.
37
A Tempo
p
6
Tpt. 2

Tpt. 1

VIRGIL THOMSON

THE PLOW THAT BROKE THE PLAINS

for Brass Quintet

Trumpet 2

ED-3826
First Printing: November 1993

G. SCHIRMER, Inc.

THE PLOW THAT BROKE THE PLAINS

19
pp
p
23
3
mp
29
33
mute
p
3
40
open
f
45
f
<
50
ff
54
mp
59
mp
p
mp
63
6
Tpt. 1
73
4   rall.
ff
mf

Ⅲ. Blues

IV. Finale

"We're Goin' to Leave Ol' Texas Now"

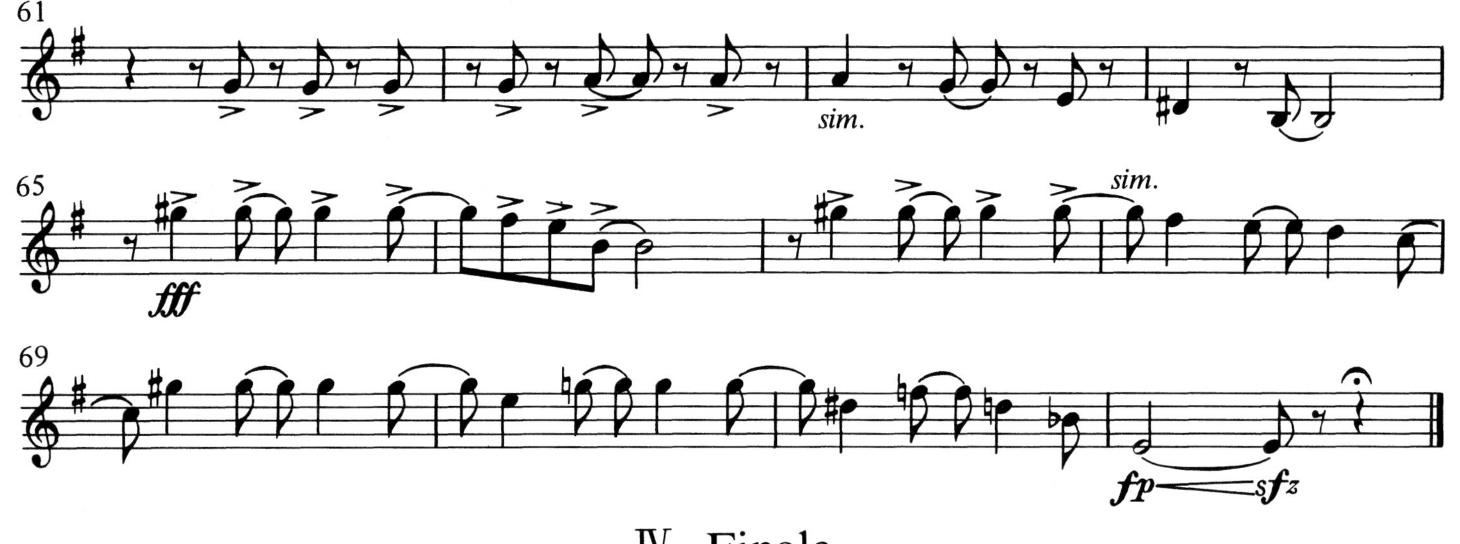

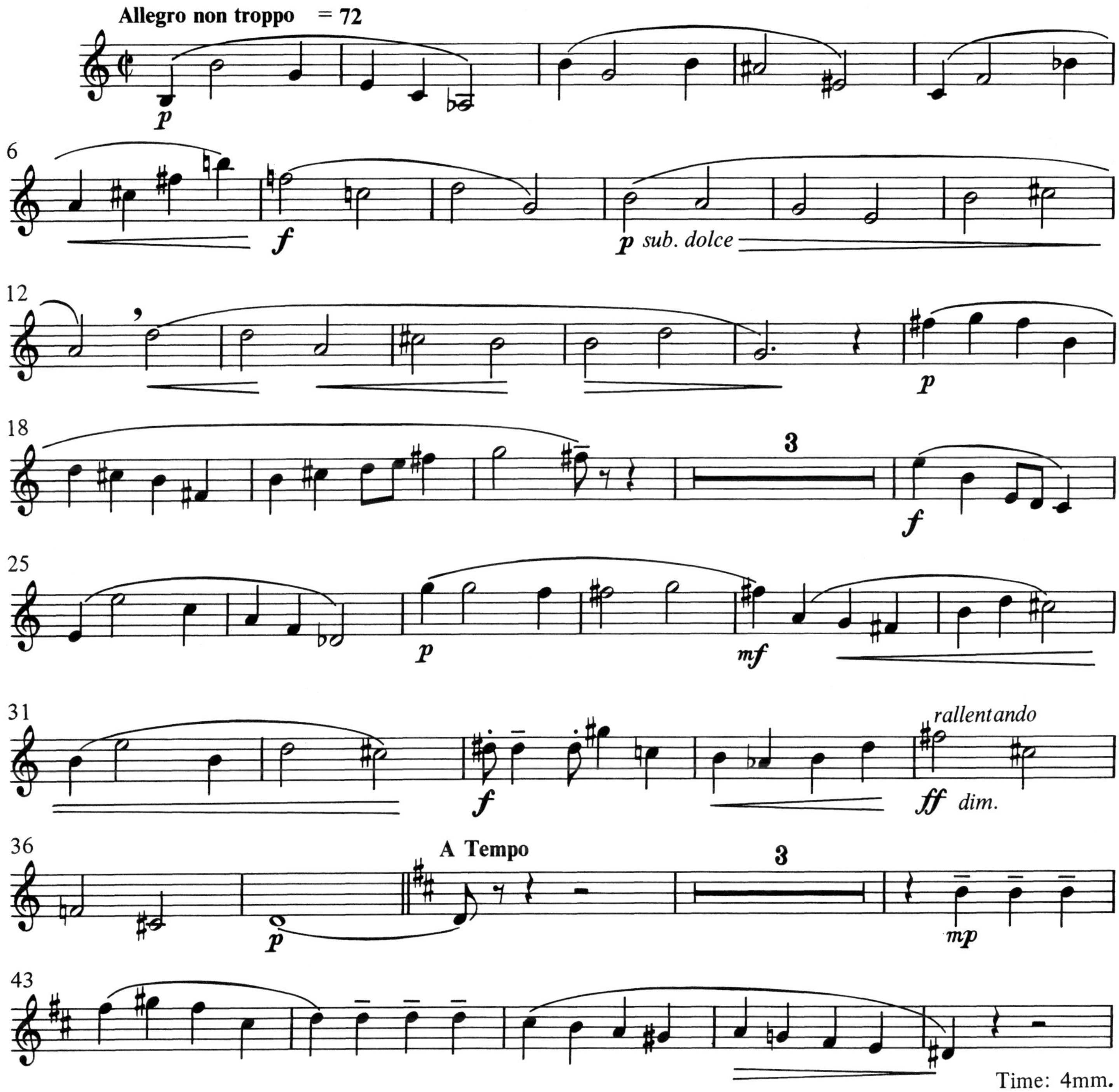

Time: 4mm.

48
4
mp
p
56
pp sub.
mf
63
3
5
mf
73
Tbn.
mf
78
f
85
ff
92
pp legato e
dolce
99
106
Un poco più lento ♩ = 60
mf molto vibr.
113
f
119
rit.
A Tempo
ff
125
rall.
fff

VIRGIL THOMSON

THE PLOW THAT BROKE THE PLAINS

for Brass Quintet

Horn

ED-3826
First Printing: November 1993

G. SCHIRMER, Inc.

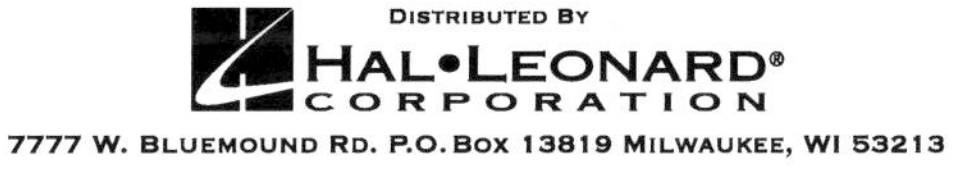
DISTRIBUTED BY
HAL•LEONARD®
CORPORATION
7777 W. BLUEMOUND RD. P.O. BOX 13819 MILWAUKEE, WI 53213

THE PLOW THAT BROKE THE PLAINS

23
27
31
3
38
42
46
51
56
61
65
69
4
77
p
p
mp
mf
mf
f
p
f
mf
p
sim.
p
f
ff
p
p

Ⅲ. Blues

♩ = 96
p
ff
f
mp
fp
mf
mp
gliss.
f
p
sim.
fltg.
fltg.
fltg.
fltg.
fp   sfz
fp   sfz
fp   sfz
fp   sfz

IV. Finale

"We're Goin' to Leave Ol' Texas Now"

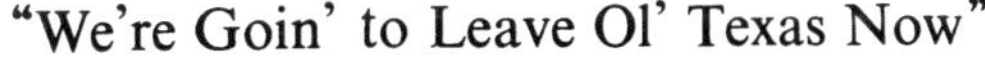

Hn.

73
81
87
93
99
Un poco piu lento ♩ = 60
7
Tpt.1
Play
mf
f
ff
mp
109
114
f
sim.
119
A tempo
rit.
ff
125
rall.
fff

VIRGIL THOMSON

THE PLOW THAT BROKE THE PLAINS

for Brass Quintet

Trombone

ED-3826
First Printing: November 1993

G. SCHIRMER, Inc.

THE PLOW THAT BROKE THE PLAINS

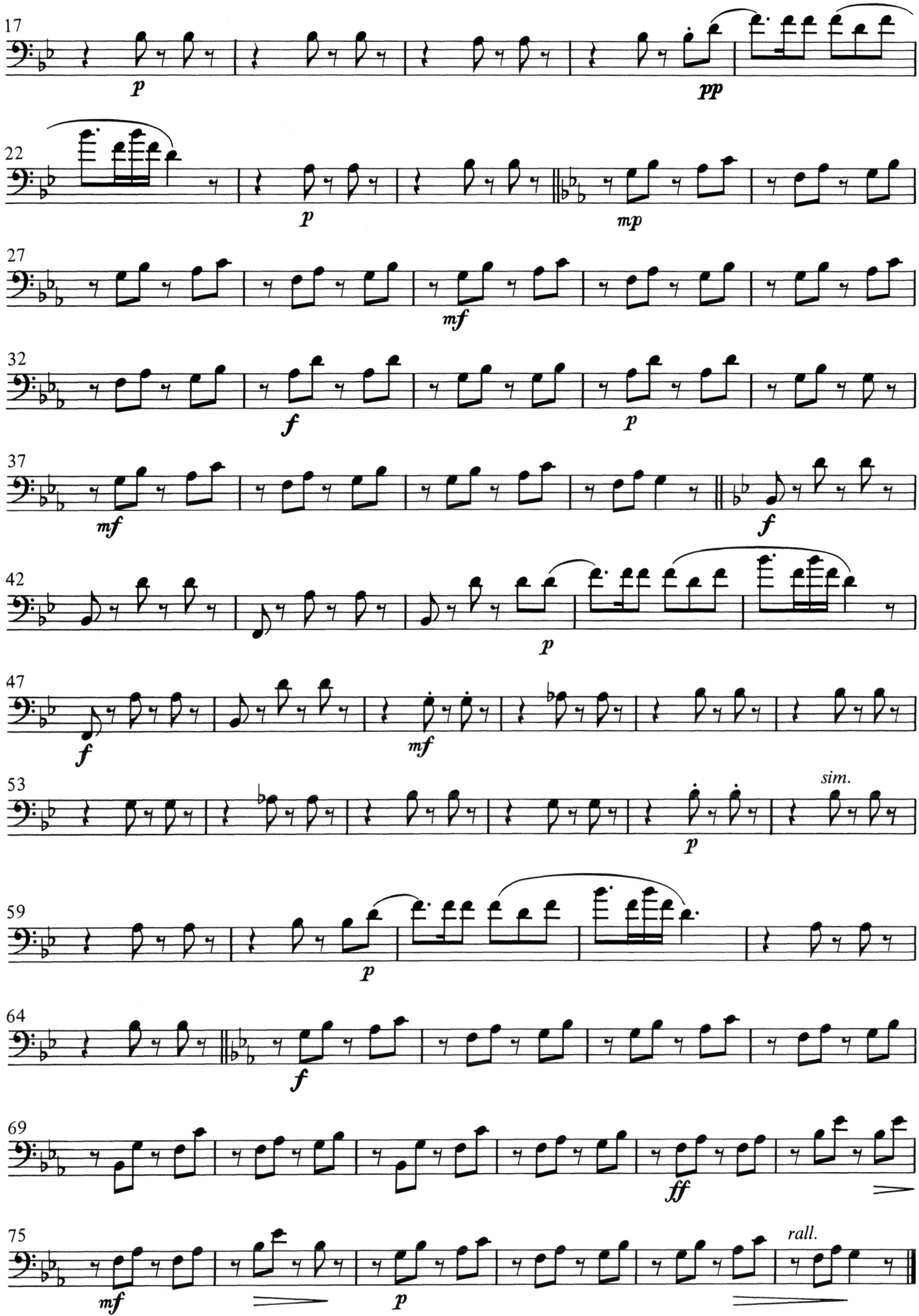

Ⅲ. Blues

Ⅳ. Finale

"We're Goin' to Leave Ol' Texas Now"

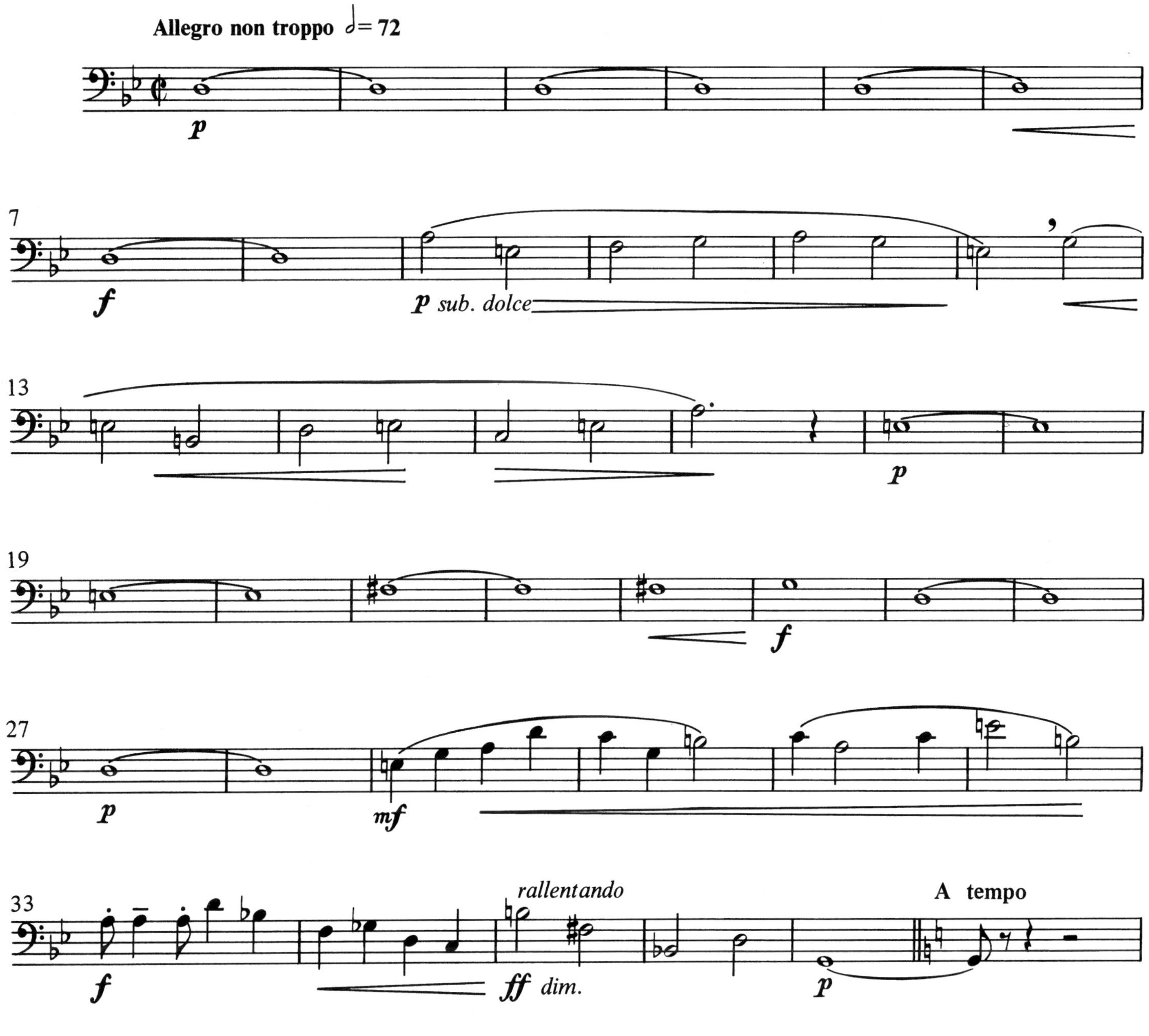

Tbn.

Un poco più lento
♩ = 60

sim.

rit.
A tempo

rall.

VIRGIL THOMSON

THE PLOW THAT BROKE THE PLAINS

for Brass Quintet

Tuba

ED-3826
First Printing: November 1993

G. SCHIRMER, Inc.

THE PLOW THAT BROKE THE PLAINS

I. Prelude

12
18
24
29
35
41
46
52
58
sim.
64
69
75
p
pp
p
mp
mf
f
p
mf
f
f
f
mf
f
f
p
f
ff
mf
p
rall.

Ⅲ. Blues

IV. Finale

"We're Goin' to Leave Ol' Texas Now"

Tuba